BRAVE NELLIE

BY

SHARALYN MORRISON-ANDREWS

ILLUSTRATED BY LUCAS RICHARDS

ISBN: 978-0-9962889-0-3
Library of Congress Control Number: 2015905980

This book was printed in the United States of America.

Published by Sharalyn Morrison-Andrews
May, 2015

I would like to dedicate this book to:

David, my wonderful and supportive husband;

all the special people and animals who have
touched my life;

those who made this story possible:
Louise, Toril, Sherry, Matt, Megan, Petey,
Kingston,

and of course,
Nellie.

BRAVE NELLIE

Once there were three dogs who lived on the beach of a beautiful island.

Their names were Buddy, Nellie and Poco.

They were the best of friends and did everything together. During the day they would run and play on the beach.

At night they would curl under a palm tree and sleep.

One day a couple named Emily and Bryce came to live on the island.

They loved dogs and soon made friends with Nellie, Buddy and Poco.

While Bryce was at work, Emily would play with the three dogs or sit quietly with them on the beach. She gave them food and water and helped them if they got sick or hurt.

After two years, it was time for Emily and Bryce to move to a new home. They were sad to leave their dog friends behind.

After thinking a long while, Nellie asked if she could go with them and live in a "forever home."

Sadly, Emily and Bryce couldn't have Nellie live with them.

They promised, however, to help Nellie find a family that could give her a "forever home."

While looking for that special family, Emily and Bryce invited Nellie to live with them.

Nellie had never lived inside a home before and she had so many new things to learn and try.

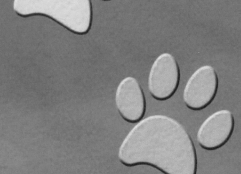

She was a very brave little doggie and tried everything that Emily and Bryce showed her.

Nellie had never walked on a hard floor or climbed up and down stairs...

She had never slept on a bed...

Nellie had never worn
a collar or walked with
a leash...

She had never walked on grass or...

been in the woods...

She had never been for a ride in a car.

Every day there were so many
new things for Nellie to learn.
With each new thing Nellie would
say to herself:

"What to do, what to do?
All so scary, all so new.
But I must try each day,
To be brave
And everything will be OK."

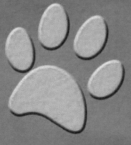

With each new thing Nellie
learned, she became braver.
Nellie started to think that
she was on a great adventure
and she became very excited.

One day Emily brought a big plastic box with a door on the front and told Nellie it was a crate.

Emily explained to Nellie that she had to learn to go inside the crate so she could ride on the airplane that would take her to her "forever home."

Nellie was very nervous. She had never been inside such a small space before.

"What to do, what to do?
All so scary, all so new.
But I must try each day,
To be brave
And everything will be OK!"

Nellie walked into the crate...
and do you know what? She really liked it!
She liked it so much that every night
she would sleep in it!
What started out as scary became fun
because Nellie was brave enough to try
something new.

Finally, the big day came when Emily, Bryce and Nellie were to leave the island for their new homes.
They got up early to say a sad good-bye to their friends, Buddy and Poco.
Then, into the car they all went for the ride to the airport.

Beep!
Beep!

For Nellie, the airport was especially
new and scary.
People were rushing everywhere, loud
announcements were being made and small
carts were constantly beeping
and whizzing by.

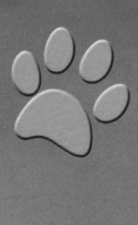

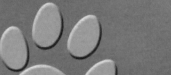

Nellie said to herself:

"What to do, what to do?
All so scary, all so new!
But I must try each day,
To be brave,
And everything will be OK!"

Emily helped Nellie into her crate for the flight home.

The crate was put on a moving belt that carried Nellie inside the airplane.

Nellie waited and suddenly the plane started to move. It moved slowly at first, then it rolled faster and faster until it felt like they were in the air!
Eventually, Nellie curled up and went to sleep.

When Nellie got off the plane, Emily and Bryce were waiting for her.

Together they all got into the car and began the long ride to Nellie's "forever home."

Everything was so different from her life on the beach. There was no sand, but everywhere she looked she saw grass.

Roads stretched for as far as Nellie could see and all around were cars and more cars!

During the long ride, Emily and Bryce told Nellie about her new family:
Katie and Andrew...

their cat, Mittens and their dog, Petey. Nellie was nervous about meeting *all* of them. She was not certain she would like living with a cat.

For the long ride, Nellie kept
saying to herself:

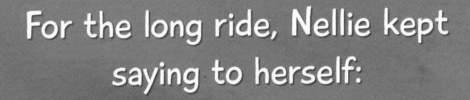

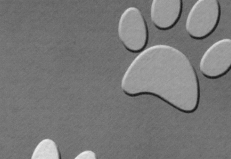

"What to do, what to do?
All so scary, all so new!
But I must try each day
To be brave,
And everything will be OK!"

Once they arrived, Nellie immediately loved her new home and "forever family"... even Mittens the cat!

It was sad to say good-bye to Emily and Bryce, but she knew that she would see them again.

Although Nellie misses her old friends, she is very, very happy in her "forever home."

So, when you face something
that is new and scary,
just remember Nellie
and say to yourself:

"What to do, what to do?
All so scary, all so new!
But I must try each day,
To be brave
And everything will be OK!"

Buddy   Nellie   Poco

I hope you have enjoyed the story about Nellie, the beach dog. It is based on a true story from events that happened during the two years that my husband and I lived in Cabarete, Dominican Republic.

Part of the profits of this book will be donated to help support the stray dogs on the north coast of the Dominican Republic.

Should you wish to contact me, you may do so at:
sharalynlovesanimals@gmail.com

Buddy, Nellie, and Poco
playing on the beach.

Nellie, Buddy, and Poco
eating on the beach.

Nellie's first night inside.

Nellie loving the crate.

Nellie sleeping in bed.

Nellie arriving in the States.

Sharalyn and Nellie in Maine.

Petey waiting for Nellie

Sherry and Nellie.

Matt and Nellie.

Megan and Nellie.

Kingston waiting for Nellie.

Nellie experienced her first winter of cold and snow in Michigan, with her new family. The following summer they moved to Arizona. Nellie's days are now spent basking in the hot Arizona sun and the love of her "forever family."

It is with great appreciation that I acknowledge the many people and pets who selflessly gave their support and encouragement to the creation of this book:

Louise Poppema, my pet communicator, whose insight into the minds of the beach dogs proved invaluable through Nellie's transition.

Judy Liggio, president of the Association of the Animals of Sosua, Inc, for walking us through the process of transporting a dog from the Dominican Republic to the United States.

Toril Brooker-Fisher for introducing me to Nellie's forever family.

Nellie's forever family, Sherry Jensen and her children, Megan and Matt Dankert, for opening their hearts and home to Nellie and making her transition from life on the beach to living with a family a smooth one.

Petey, Sherry's beloved rescue dog, whose acceptance of Nellie made this story possible.

Kingston, the cat, for accepting another dog into her domain.

Tom and Char Dickens and Sarah Winslow for their encouragement to tell the story.

Kathy Brodsky, an accomplished author of children's books, whose support and encouragement guided me through the publishing process.

Brave Nellie's knowledgable editor, Julie Stephano, and talented illustrator, Lucas Richards.

Elise Galgano for her wonderful photos for the biographies.

My husband, David, who supported me through Nellie's transition and the writing of this book.

Sharalyn grew up in Hallowell, Maine and was bitten by the "travel bug" at a very young age. While she loved to travel as a young woman, it was her marriage to David, whose job frequently takes them out of the country, that made travel a vital part of her life.

Over the years, Sharalyn has enjoyed writing by keeping a journal and most recently, a blog. It wasn't until Nellie came into her life, however, that she truly felt she had a story to share.

You can follow Sharalyn on her website at www.sharalynlovesanimals.com. When not traveling, Sharalyn and her husband make their home in Maine.

Lucas grew up in Cape Elizabeth, Maine. His aptitude as an artist emerged early in life. One could find him drawing on anything he could reach in his family's home.

More recently, he's a graduate from the University of Maine with a degree in New Media and Studio Art. His studies and passion for travel have allowed him to visit some of the world's best art museums, experiences that influence his style today.

You can follow Lucas on his website at www.lucas-richards.com.